THE
BATTLE
FOR ME

A SURVIVORS STORY

M'SHAIRI BREE

ISBN: 978-1-7353960-4-0

Published By: Awaken U Publishing

www.JanayRoberson.com

Contents

ACKNOWLEDGEMENTS

Before I thank anyone, I must first give thanks and honor to my Savior and Lord Jesus Christ. I would not be alive or able to finish this book without Him.

To my praying grandmother, Emily, who did not live to see this in print. I did it, Grandma! I am o.k. I love you, my little old lady.

To my mother, our relationship is definitely unique. Through it all, you have always been there. You showed me how to build my foundation on solid rock. For that, I will be forever grateful.

To my twins, Dem Babies, Mommy loves you more than life itself. You two are the greatest blessing God has given me. I fought to bring you into this world, and I will fight for you until I am no longer in this world. You have taught me the meaning of unconditional love. You have taught me how to open myself up to love and to lead in a way to be followed. I do this so you know you can do anything you put your mind to. That you build your life on the foundation of the Word and Jesus.

My sisters: Korbi, Kauritha, Melody, and Christina. Lord, where would I be without you ladies. Each relationship almost didn't start, but somehow we found our rhythm in life and laughter. Each of you plays a pivotal and crucial role in my life. I love each relationship and the uniqueness each has. Korbi, my baby birthday twin you have literally walked me through the writing of this book and my next 3 books. You never let me forget who I am. Kauritha, you always keep me grounded and let me be me in the totality of all that I am. I would not be here without you. Christina, ma'am, I love our relationship. You came along right on time. I know it's time for another trip. And definitely not last or least. My twin Melody. Maam, from the day you laid me out, I knew somehow we would be connected. I am so glad, honored, and excited for our future. Sisters in Christ and sisters in life. Ladies, I love me some you and you already know what that means.

My brothers; Darrin, KD, Tim. Listen. You men mean so much to me. Darrin is my only blood brother and you can't tell us anything different. I love you so much. We lost some years, but I am glad we are here and moving forward. I look forward to the future and our growth. KD and Tim. Oh, the stories that can be told. Two individual friendships have formed into a tribe. KD, whoever would have thought from National to now. When is the next movie night? Tim, I don't even know. From Scandal to Homecoming. I still have no words. Family night has gotten me through hard times more than you ever knew. I love you all.

Godfather Isaac, Godmother Beck, Godmother Mary, Godmother Boot, Godfather Price, Aunt Dorothy. You all meant so much to me. I cherish the childhood memories I have. Some died when I was young, some died in my adult years. None of you got to see this, but all of you are a credit to this. I love you and miss you. See you again.

There are so many more people that mean so much to me I can not say thank you to them all. Different times, different seasons, different people have walked me through my life. You know who you are, family and friends, I love you.

INTRODUCTION

The hardest thing to do is wait. I've been waiting and waiting and still nothing. I want to give up!

I believe we have all made these statements at one point or another. I know I have. Plenty of times. However, giving up was not an option and it can't be for you either. You may be saying to yourself, "...but I don't know how hard it is or how long it's been?" Well, let me show you how you know you can make it too. I wasn't waiting for a few days or even weeks, try years. Yes, that's right..YEARS... The most trying time of my life. Out of my pain, my purpose was born.

I feel as if I have been fighting all my life. In retrospect, it seems that I have. Whether I am fighting physical or spiritual battles or even both at the same time. As I sit here having made it out of this battle, I sometimes feel as if it was a lifetime ago and yet, it feels like yesterday at the same time. So, let's start with where I am, how I got here, and finally how I got out.

So, where is here? Who am I?

Who I Am

Gasping. Clawing. Fighting to breathe. How heavy you now feel on top of me.

The light is dimming. I'm fighting within', please don't let this darkness overtake me.

This can't be it...my story is incomplete.

But wait ....I can see the light now shining all around me,

Sweating and panting

Inhaling deeply, I start coughing uncontrollably

There you sit laughing at me.

What seemed like hours, only minutes it lasted

having become complacent, I took life for granted.

See this isn't about sex or all that wonderful mess

This is about when so-called love leaves you with nothing left

This is for those that go through every day,

Not realizing how we got here, and not sure how to get away.

For some of us, it's a nightmare that we're living

no fairytales and sometimes no happy endings

See that was the first time he put me to sleep... but, not in a way that was pleasurable for me.. but by a chokehold you see. And this wasn't the first time he had put his hands on me, but this was the day that I finally woke up to see

That this can't be love and I can't be ashamed... because he is to blame

but by me staying, I also must lay claim

It started at 18 with a hard slap, by 21 I was so lost, still fighting over this cat.

Young and confused. Molested and abused. No strong bonds to those who were to protect me, when they were the ones who were the first to neglect me.

See he was smooth ... and even kind of fine...and he wore me down over time

It was so subtle, I didn't even notice, until one day my life was out of focus...

Knowing I needed better, Knowing I deserved better.

But knowing and doing was something different altogether

I even had those that said, "But girl he really loves you."

Well, if this is your love, then what the hell happened to you?

Because when did abuse become a form of saying, "Baby, I love you."

Yeah, I lived good and had it all it seemed, but that still didn't stop the threats, the fights, or keep him coming home to only me.

So years passed and I don't know who I became, not knowing myself or even my own name.

For my freedom, I would have to fight...It would take me some time, but this is what I did for me I had to find...

So, you look at me now and all you may see

is a smile on my lips, the sashay in my hips, the thickness in these thighs...but look deep into my eyes.

Take a good look at me...the delicate parts you may not immediately see...

I fought hard to be here, I fight it every day

not just for myself, but for all those in harm's way.

So now here I stand. I will gladly take your hand and let you know exactly who I now am.

It took me six months to write that poem and it took me a year before I would ever speak those words out loud. That is not something I read about or have a passion for, it's what I lived through. I was still living under a threat when I wrote it.

I had done the unthinkable and therefore I was to be punished. However, leaving was no longer an option. The fights had become almost regular at this point. After a couple of times of being choked to sleep and threats made to my family, the rise in his voice or a threat of violence, was all it took to be sure I fell in line. When did my life become this? How am I separated and still confined? One word. Fear. The scariest thing there is. The funny thing about fear is it will either paralyze or push you. I had been paralyzed most of my adult life by it, but now it would help push me. I had to push past it. Not for me though, but for the beautiful children that I was blessed to be able to raise.

The funny thing is I had changed my mind about having kids. Before I got pregnant, I decided that I didn't want kids anymore. Though most of my life I wanted kids, I even said I wanted twins, but had recently changed my mind and was planning to get my tubes tied. He already had kids with other women and I knew kids would change our relationship or probably would be the end of us. In a twist of fate, it was.

Yet God had a different plan and I had the twins I told God I wanted a few years before. Now, I had to do what was necessary for them to live a life of peace and be better than both of us. I refused to let my children grow up thinking it was ok to live like this. He could do whatever to me. I had chosen this life and was used to it, but my children did not. What type of mother would I be if I didn't do everything for their betterment?

So how did I even end up here? Playing a live game of chess trying to outwit my cunning opponent. It didn't start out bad. It started out nice. We had built a unique friendship in high school. In college, things changed. Before I start there, let's go back to the beginning of the story.

THE BACKGROUND

If there ever was a time in which I could say my destiny must be tied to a place, then it would be Huntsville, AL. When I think of Huntsville, it seems as if the devil made it his top priority to make sure I would have nothing to say from the moment I got here. I had not long been diagnosed with asthma in Arizona. It was well controlled until I arrived. It has been said that the Native Americans have called this place the valley of death because of it being like a basin for pollen and dander to settle, which makes it a problem, especially for those with allergies. Well, I am diagnosed with allergies and asthma. In my first year here, I was in the emergency room almost every weekend. I would come in and they would know me by name. It was also my first experience of attending a predominantly black school.

At first, I was excited, I thought it would be great. That feeling quickly dissipated and was replaced with sadness and anxiety. It was here I was introduced to bullying. You name it, I was picked on for it. Being new, standing much shorter than most of my peers, and underdeveloped. Wearing pigtails. Using correct English. Talking "white" as they called it. Dressing preppy, and being called "Rudolph" due to allergies, did not make for a pleasant experience. Not to mention, I loved school and I loved to learn. My love of learning got me tested for early promotion but it also got me labeled a teachers' pet. I hated school. I hated Alabama. In a time of Salt N Pepa, (the rap duo) and ripped jeans with funky short hairstyles, I did not fit in at all. My mother was not trying to help me conform.

I was more of an Ashley Banks, (character from the Fresh Prince of Bel-Air, 90s sitcom). However, there were a few bright spots. I managed to make a few friends, one I still talk to this day. I wouldn't have made it without them. We are not as close as I would like to be, but I understand the seasons. There was one day I will never forget. It was field day, I think, a relaxing day. We were outside and in the gym most of the day, close to the end of the year. Me and a guy Bill had been trading jokes back and forth for a while. I was holding my own. Had a nice little crowd around. It got time to go back to class, to get ready to leave. I remember trying to let it go and be done.

He had to have the last say. I can't tell you what he said or what my reply was, but it was simple, sweet, and had the entire hallway burst out laughing at him. Nothing but oohs and ahhs and how I had played him. I'll never forget it, I felt like a champ. I was getting pats on the back and felt like finally, it was over. He stopped at his locker and I kept on to mine, right at the end of the hall before the double doors to the lunchroom. I am putting in my locker combination when all of a sudden, WHACK! He smacked the fire out of me! I left my face facing to my left and quickly contemplated my next move. He walked away feeling redeemed. I quietly put my stuff in my locker, shut it, walked back up to his locker, and punched him in his face, knocking his glasses off. The fight now ensued.

Now he has me by a few inches and a good 15 pounds or more, but now I am mad. We are trading blows and getting pushed by the crowd through the doors into the lunchroom so that the school police officer won't see us. Now I have my hands around his neck, choking the snot out of him. They are telling me to let him go and I'm trying to understand what has gotten into him. His face is turning red and it takes a few kids to pull me off of him, but not without leaving claw marks on his neck. He is choking and trying to breathe and in that moment, I calmed down and I look to him and say, *"Don't you ever in your life put your hands on me again or the next time, I will break more than your glasses."*

I have no idea who I was at that moment or that I had that in me. As I walked back to my locker, people were parting like the Red Sea. Girls who had been the source of my torment, came up to say, *"Hey you did well defending yourself Lil' bit. You real cool."* At that moment, it was interesting seeing the fact that they are now a little concerned because they realized I have been drastically underestimated.

I said, "Don't 'congrats' me now. No one else was trying to help me and don't act like you like me. You can respect me for finally standing up for myself because it wasn't for you. Let's be clear, I am done being anyone's joke and if you can't call me by my name we can go toe-to-toe right now."

"Naw Lil' bit, we good. No harm."

I will never forget those words. I think we only had like two weeks left of school, but I didn't have any more problems after that. Most of those people I never saw again. The nickname did stick with me though.

In 7th grade, I was in a different school. I never told my mom about the incident. She always worked to keep me calm and nonviolent. Although she told me to always defend myself and if I ever get jumped, get one, preferably the leader, and beat the brakes off of them. As a child around two, my mom realized that this "baby Hulk" is going to get mad one day and hurt someone because I didn't realize my own strength. I think that is why my mom always worked to keep me calm. In doing so, she also kept me afraid for a while. I realize now I am a fighter by nature. I was born fighting. I only had to change who my opponents were. I would soon come to realize how much of a fighter I was.

After moving here, I started to be molested on a regular basis and two men would violate me for years before I would say anything. And when I did finally, out of anger, speak my truth, I was not believed. This would leave a wound in me that would go unhealed for over 20 years. This would also set me up to be prey for certain predators.

IN THE BEGINNING

I met him in 7th grade, he was an 8th grader. He was a star basketball player with a penchant for fighting I heard. He was well-liked, but not cute to me. I was talking to his cousin. I thought he was crazy. 7th grade was pretty much the same as the 6th more bullying and being made fun of and not as many status symbols here as in 6th grade. This may be the difference between the city and the county at this time. I wouldn't see him again for three years. In my freshman year in high school, things took a drastic turn. I had met a guy, Tom, my best friend's cousin who graduated high school. We liked each other and he never pressured me for sex. We would kiss, but that was it. My parents were not too pleased to know he had been coming to the house to see me. They didn't understand. However, in my hurt and anger, I finally divulged that he wasn't the one to be worried about, but they should be more concerned with my molester.

They were shocked and didn't want to believe me. I only told them of one, it didn't make any sense to tell of the other one, since they didn't believe me about the first person. After I told them what was happening, I was taken to counseling, to see a Psychologist and my pastors. At this point, I had nothing more to say since I wasn't believed. This would further isolate me to myself. The other molester would continue for another year until he would rape me when I was in 11th grade.

After that, I got better at evading and not ending up anywhere alone with him. To this day, he admits his love for me and how he has loved me since I was young.

In my freshman year, I also met a guy I knew would be my boyfriend and take my virginity, Mike. I first briefly met Mike in 8th grade at a basketball game. He played for a rival school and I thought he was cute. We barely exchanged hellos, but I was accused of being the reason he missed a free throw or two. He reminded me of this when we met again in high school. We clicked immediately and became instant friends. He bet me we would sleep together before we graduated. I denied it, of course, and took the bet. I won the bet. We didn't sleep together. However, it broke my heart when he showed up one day and was talking to another girl. We still remained best friends. However, our friendship would be tested and ultimately would fail.

In my 10th grade year, I was still trying to fit in and find my way. In the first part of the year, I landed in ICU on a ventilator for three days. I was in the ICU for five days total and a regular room for two. It was an asthma attack. This changed my perspective, as I sat there fighting to live. I knew that prayer, God, and those great doctors saved me. I had been raised in church and my faith was strong. I went to school with a different attitude. The pettiness didn't matter to me. My patience with foolishness and fakeness was wearing thin. So I adopted an "I don't care," and standoffish attitude. It didn't appear that many of my classmates were genuine.

Every time I thought I had a friend, they turned out to be a foe. My so-called best friend from 7th and 8th grades turned out to be enemy number one. She set me up to be jumped, talked about me behind my back, bullied me like the others, and even stole pages out of my diary. This turned into a hatred for school. I absolutely hated it. I can't look back and remember any good times, only tortuous times. From being picked on, to stand up for myself, and being labeled a "riot starter." Oh how far I would change from the happy, quiet, wanting to get along with people, non-violent type; to the angry, chip on my shoulder, no-nonsense, ready to fight girl.

This is where thoughts of depression and suicide started. Body issues that would lead to anorexia and bulimia started here. Either I didn't eat at all or if I did, I would throw it up to be sure I kept my small waist and flat stomach. This was the one thing I could control when it seemed as if I didn't have control over much else in my life.

I have always been shy and being the new kid at every school for the last four years didn't help. High School further drove me into my shell. Here is where I discovered that the girls were wicked and the guys were sneaky. I always seemed to get along with guys more than girls. It was less drama. It was early in my 10th grade that I lost my virginity to a guy I was talking to, Carl.

One day after school, he took my virginity at his friend's house. It hurt. Blood was everywhere and it wasn't anything like they talked about in school, however, I felt like a real woman. We broke up about two weeks later. I wouldn't have sex again for seven more months with another guy who had been after me for two years. It was better and so a month after that, I began to have sex regularly with him. As crazy as it was, we never dated, but became close. He was always sweet to me and we talked about everything. He doesn't realize how his friendship helped me through high school. Late in my 10th-grade year, I got a phone call from Cass. He called an associate of mine from church by accident. They started talking and somehow my name came up and she gave him my number. I had not long gotten my own phone line in my room. We started talking only as friends catching up.

I couldn't date and leave my house like other teenagers, so our friendship grew from a lot of late-night talks. It would also be in this year, that I would once again have to take a stand for myself. This year my best friend and former friend got into it. It wasn't my fight initially, but it soon became my fight. Mya used to be my best friend, but we had been enemies for a few years and I had finally had enough. This day I ended the torture. I got angry and was ready to fight. I went looking for her and found her and her crew in the lunchroom. I walked and asked her what she said, however, Gina and a few friends are trying to stop me. I am literally dragging them as I am determined to get to this chick.

Finally, in a group effort, five of them literally picked me up and took me out of the lunchroom. They put me down and I am calm. She runs past me to her sister and play brother. I go back into the building and her play brother asks me what happened. I looked him in the face and explained to him that she needs to stop running her mouth, especially if she can't back it up. And now people are like if you fight her, I want to fight her friend. My thoughts were, *"Umm no I don't care about your beef you are on your own."* So I get called to the office and I'm being accused of possibly inciting a riot. *"No sir, I don't have anything to do with that."* I didn't get in trouble as long as I let it end there. I told the vice-principal and her that I am fine, but if she got something to say she better say it to my face. I don't care if she likes me or not, I don't like her and that is fine.

I am tired of her running her mouth and if someone comes and tells me anything else, next time I am punching first and asking questions later. I am sure she despised me, however, I never had another problem with her or her clique after that. I actually never had another problem with anyone else. Gina and I would soon become enemies as well by the end of the year. We would almost come to blows the following year, but having seen my anger first-hand, she would always be sure that she was nowhere around when it was out that I was looking for her or, she would quickly leave my presence. I would also no longer be friends with Mike by the end of the year.

Summer had now come and Cass offered to come see me. He had dropped out of school to take care of his son. He joined the family business to provide for his child. He offered to take me to his house, one he lived in by himself. He was 17 and I was 15. He had a girlfriend or three and I had guys I would date, but we didn't care. He was funny and had gotten cuter and had money now. My junior year started and sometimes, he would take me to school. And so this would continue through my senior year. I graduated at 17 and when I went to college, we continued to see each other. He now had three kids.

He had begun to make small threats if I didn't see him when he wanted and he started just showing up on campus. It was one night I had come from a friend's house when he popped up and surprised me after I parked my car. I knew better than to get out of the car, so I kept the doors locked and rolled down the window a little. He hit me like three times and then was gone. I was so surprised and shocked. I went to my room and didn't even know how to process it. We never talked about it. He began to change. On my 18th birthday, I found out I was pregnant. I was devastated. Remember the guy Tom from my freshman year in high school? Well, we continued to see each other off and on through high school. I would sneak out to see him and in my junior year, he left for the military. We still communicated and were still friends. He came back to see me. He asked me to marry him, but I was pregnant. We both concluded that this is where we would end. He left heartbroken and I was numb.

We would talk a few more times and then lose contact until I ran into him 12 years later. I was crushed. I wasn't sure I wanted to marry him, but I felt like the decision was taken away from me. I wasn't even sure I was going to keep the baby. I had been taking care of babies since I was five years old. It was second nature to me. I was always in the nursery at church, babysitting, and keeping my nieces and nephews. I knew I would get married and have children young, but this was not the plan.

Cass and I were not exclusive, I wasn't married or engaged and I wasn't even sure I wanted a baby by him or if I wanted to be with him. I knew my parents would be disappointed. I was scared and never felt so alone. He convinced me that this was not the time to have more babies. I wasn't ready for that life change and didn't think I could do it on my own. So he took me to have my first abortion. The first appointment I made, he didn't come get me in time and I had to cancel. I thought about keeping my baby, but I was still scared, so I rescheduled and he was on time that day. He dropped me off. My first stop would be for an ultrasound to be sure I was far enough along and to see the location of the baby. I'll never forget hearing the heartbeat.

With no time to process, I was rushed up and ushered into another room to wait. A room full of women my age and older, as we bonded over the decision we made waiting on our name to be called and passing around crackers for the nausea most of us had as a result of morning sickness.

I sat quietly trying to process the decision I was making. I wanted to run out of the building, but then my name was called. I knew this was wrong, this went against everything I believed in. This was murder. I was scared. I laid on the table. The doctor came in, said, "You will feel a strong cramp." I heard the suction machine start. I closed my eyes and it was done in less than five minutes. The nurse helped me up, gave me a pad to put on, and ushered me to the final waiting room. I had to sit for 30 minutes to be sure I wasn't going to lose too much blood. They gave me more crackers and water, I felt sick to my stomach, but I was not going to cry in front of these people so I went numb.

After my waiting time, I was allowed to leave. I called Cass after the procedure was over, so he would know when to come get me. I went downstairs and ran into a guy from high school. We briefly spoke, but there was no concern of either one of us saying we ran into each other at this place. On the way back to the dorm, he stopped at Burger King to get me something to eat. I wasn't hungry, I only wanted to lay down. He dropped me off and said he would be back later. I went upstairs, laid down, and cried. He came to me later and said I kind of wished you didn't do it. Those words would haunt me, that I didn't fight hard enough to keep my baby. I spiraled into a deep depression. I barely made it to classes and I was unfocused. A few days later, my friend Harmony found out she was pregnant and her due date was a few weeks after mine. I almost lost my mind.

I supported and was there for her, but watching her growing belly only reminded me of the emptiness in mine. She had a son. He always holds a special place in my heart and some days I wonder what my son would be like now. I began drinking more heavily and smoking weed. I had been drinking since the age of 16. Anything to numb my feelings and stop my mind from thinking. Now I needed more to continue to be numb. I passed two classes and flunked two classes. I wanted to take a break, but my mother said no. That I was distracted and needed to focus. I hadn't told her about the abortion. One night when I was having a hard time dealing with my loss, I finally told her I had a miscarriage because I couldn't bring myself to tell her I had an abortion. She said it was ok. She told me to get back on track, my time will come at the right time.

Cass and I got into it, as I was packing up my dorm. He slapped me so hard, my left ear still rings to this day. We were still mainly off and on and now I heard he was seeing Gina, my former best friend from high school. I was devastated and angry. This would start a tug-of-war that would last the next 10 years. The next few years were off and on with Cass. Gina would get the brunt of his anger, frustration, and blows. I would mostly get the good times, although the verbal and emotional abuse began to pick up at this point. He was in and out of jail a lot. It was also during this time that I would begin to walk into one of my spiritual gifts at church. We were at the beginning of a revival. The next semester started and I was now living at home. I would get up and go to work most days at Blockbuster Video, but most days were a haze.

I woke up to a drink and ended my day drunk and/or high. I flunked out again. I couldn't focus. I was consumed with guilt and trying to keep Cass, although I was seeing other guys myself. There was one guy, in particular, an older guy Roger.

He was nine years older than me. He heard all about my problems with Cass and Gina yet he still wanted to be with me. It kind of worked, we both had issues. He wasn't necessarily over his ex either. I decided that I could no longer stay in my parent's house and had found an ad for a girl looking for a roommate. Lala was 28 and I was 18, but we clicked. I gave her my deposit on a Sunday, went home, and told my parents I was moving out and they couldn't stop me.

I had never seen my mom so mad at me before. She told me to go and leave the keys to the house. I packed up my clothes and was gone by the weekend. Things with my parents hadn't been good for a while. It would be years before we even began to make it right. One night while at my house, Roger tells me I'm pregnant. I ask how. He says he knows. He has had cravings and is sleepy a lot. I think he is crazy. He bets me and I take a test. Almost a year to the day that I had my abortion, I was pregnant again. Ralph was excited. I was again devastated. How could I let this happen again a year apart? He wanted to keep it. I wasn't sure he was the father, further complicating issues. I knew I was more careful and had taken my pills. I was still numb from the first abortion and I did not have the energy to go through a what-if.

Cass would have a fit and I didn't want to break Ralph's heart by carrying a baby and then finding out that the baby may not be his. So rather than wait to break his heart I broke it early. I told Cass I was pregnant and he was all too willing to take me back to the clinic. He had now gotten married to Gina and wasn't trying to tell her he had gotten me pregnant. So once again, I had another abortion. Ralph was inconsolable. It took him weeks to be able to look at me again. He eventually got over it, but we were never the same. He really wanted to be a father. We stayed together and later that year we got engaged. I was so numb. I don't even remember the details of the second abortion. I wasn't over the first one and couldn't process this one. I decided to get on the Depo-Provera as birth control, so I wouldn't have to deal with this again. I made up my mind that I was not going to get pregnant again. I was drinking and smoking even more. Me and my roommate were having so much fun. Sometimes you would have thought I was the oldest. I had taken off a semester and in the summer, I decided to go back to school. Now I was a full-time student with a full-time job. I was still broken and yet continuing on. I was still going to church only not as consistently. My faith was still at the core of who I was and there were times in quiet moments I would call on God.

One day that summer, I was at church having a hard time. One of our evangelists came up to pray for women who had lost a child, had problems getting pregnant, miscarried, or had an abortion. I wasn't going to go up. I didn't want everyone to know, but I was in so much hurt and pain. I finally went up. I couldn't stop the tears from falling. As soon as she got to me, she hugged me and whispered, "Oh honey, I am so sorry, but God showed me and told me to tell you don't worry. Your son is fine and sitting with Jesus. God's got him. He is ok and I will see him again. Forgive yourself. He has forgiven you. I literally fell to my knees. I was so relieved and felt like such a weight had been lifted off of me. I could not stop crying. It was close to the end of service, so I went to my car, sat there, and cried for at least 15 minutes before I could drive home. I went home and slept. I finally had some peace.

God continued to minister to me and I knew I would see my son again. I would get another chance to be his mom. This would also free me to now be able to hear more from God. Revival had hit the teens and youth. Joan and I were on the front lines moving into our calling, hearing from God, and walking into the prophetic. As much as my life was a mess, God was still using me. I was so on fire for God and He was moving mightily. Unfortunately, it wouldn't last very long. Even as we were falling in love with God, our lives were still spiraling out of control in other ways. Cass was still lingering around, Ralph and I were fighting to stay together. I was still looking for other options and still drinking and smoking. Depression still had a hold of me and I still had my eating issues and now I was working out like crazy. One night, Jess, my friend from high school, came to see me.

Me and Cass had gotten into it. Jess and I went to the garage to take her home and Cass appeared out of nowhere. Jess was yelling for me to get in the car and before I knew it, Cass was putting his hands on me. A few quick blows and then he was choking me. Jess was screaming and dialing 911. He let me go and ran off. Jess was so upset. She didn't care for Cass before and now she detested him. She stayed with me until the police came. I talked to the officer, but I wasn't going to press charges. I did not want to deal with the courts. Cass backed off for a while, but not for long.

After that, I didn't even care about guys. I played them before they could play me. School and work took up a lot of time. This time around, I was committed and focused on making good grades and getting my degree. In September of that year, my roommate Lala told me that her Reserves unit was being activated and she was being sent to Bosnia for six months. Wait what? Well, we decided that I would stay in the townhouse and she would send her half of the rent. Life began to settle down. Cass was back in jail, and Ralph and I had broken up. A few months after my roommate came back, I moved out to my own apartment. It wasn't much, but it was mine. I was now in school and working two jobs, but I loved it.

THE BREAKDOWN

Cass got out and of course, looked me up. At first, things were fine, but one night when a friend was leaving my apartment and he was coming up, he exploded. I couldn't understand how a married man should be concerned with a single woman's dealings? This didn't make sense to me, but to him, I was his and he unleashed a fury of body shots on me. Fist after fist. This was the longest 10 minutes of my life. Cass was jealous and territorial. I kept telling myself I could deal with this. I wanted to love the best parts of him and that would be my downfall. The next day he came with flowers and an apology. He left a song on my voicemail that would come to be our song. He wore me down and once again I was hooked. He was in the process of buying a truck, so he talked me into using my name and his money. I figured since it was only my name, it was okay. He will pay for it and it will help my credit. And I know him, he will pay it off early. My friend Jess thought I was a fool after calling her crying one night, after seeing Cass and his wife in the mall and being ignored.

I needed my friend, but my friend couldn't stand to see me be a fool. She brushed me off. I took it personally and was offended. Like everyone else, I felt that she had turned her back on me and our relationship was never the same. At that moment, I didn't realize why, but 20 years later, I would. She couldn't stand to see her best friend continuously hurt by someone that wasn't going to change and was only getting worse. She kept telling me to leave and I wouldn't, so if I wanted to stay, she didn't want to have a front-row seat to the impending train wreck she knew was coming. I now understand that, but back then I was furious.

Cass found a way to run off most guys who would try to get serious with me. One night I had a date and he refused to leave and threatened to follow me. I had to cancel the date. What he didn't know was most of my friends already knew and were ok with it for the time. I had now moved again, this time into a house. I had made friends with a guy at the place where I paid for my pager. One day Cass calls and says to meet him at my house for lunch. I get home and walk-in. He greets me with a hug and a kiss. He goes for my glasses and I'm like what are you doing? He says I want to see you. As I am thinking *aww*, all of a sudden, he punches me in the face. He is asking me about the guy from the pager company all the while beating me senseless.

Now I was being dragged around the living room, like a rag doll, as he pummeled my face and body with his fists. He gets on top of me and puts a plastic bag around my head trying to suffocate me. I'm frantically fighting to get him off to no avail. He removes the bag, punches me some more, and puts it back over my head while choking me at the same time. He is telling me he ought to kill me, but he won't because he loves me. As he finally gets off of me, he tells me he had my home phone line tapped.

Over the last couple of weeks, he had all his house phones tapped and had mine done too. As I am choking on my own blood, all I am thinking about is survival and if he is done beating me. I try to get to the phone and I see he has removed and hidden the headset to the phone. This starts another round of beatings. Finally, he stops. It's been at least 30 minutes and I can barely see out of one eye. He tells me to go clean up, so we can go to the pager company and I can go back to work. Blood is everywhere on the carpet and on the walls. I go upstairs to my bathroom and look at my bloodied and bruised face and think how am I going to go back to work looking like this?

When he goes downstairs to get something, I run to the phone in my bedroom and the headset is removed from that one as well. However, it has a speaker button. I turn the volume down, hit the speaker, and dial 911. I make sure they pick up, hold on the line, whisper help me, and then hang up. I knew they would call back, but the phone didn't even ring. As I am trying to clean myself up, police come knocking at the door. I try to run to the door and he grabs me and pulls me into the office and covers my mouth. Telling me to shut up and don't send him to jail. He is begging me and all I can think of is not dying here. I start kicking the wall as hard as I can. The police hear this and say if we don't let them in, they are breaking the door down and coming in. He lets me go, begs me to not say anything, and goes and hides.

I open the door and they immediately call for backup, pull out weapons and call for him to come out. One officer stays with me while the other searches the house. They find him in one of the closets. They asked me what happened and to press charges and I am numb and defensive. I want him *and* them gone. My face began to swell. They find the headsets to the phones underneath the couch. They found out my mom worked at the hospital and called her and told her to come to my house. They figured she would talk some sense into me, but what they didn't know was that me and my mom were still on the outs. The cops informed me that since it is obvious I have been beaten up, by the law they will arrest him and charge him with domestic violence, especially given the amount of blood on his shirt and hands.

My mom comes and they convince me to let her take me to the hospital to be evaluated. I called my job and lied and told them I was in a car accident, the airbag deployed and had me pretty banged up. I got to the hospital and my girl Harmony was working. She took one look at me and burst out crying. I was trying to hide my face and put ice on it. I had a concussion and a cut under my eye, but I would be fine. Harmony looked at me and said, "Girl, he's wrong, but you know he loves you, right?!" I could have stabbed her in her throat at that moment. I said, "Yeah...whatever." I didn't have much to say to anyone. My mom spent the night with me. Cass's mom came to get his car and stuff. She looked at me pitifully, but that was all.

She knew what it was like because Cass's father would beat her, however, her allegiance was to her son and I knew that. I had to sleep sitting up because it was too painful to lie down and I had a concussion. It didn't matter, I didn't get any sleep that night. The next day was worse. Me and my mom barely spoke. I told her I didn't want to hear what she had to say. She made sure I had my locks changed the next day though. It was a Friday, so I was off for the weekend. I was in such shock, I didn't know what to do. However, Cass had bailed out on Friday and by Saturday he was already calling and apologizing. He had finally broken me and he knew it. He laid back, but the next week was the Superbowl and so he convinced me to go out of town with him to Nashville to watch the game with his cousin. I remember being so jumpy and skittish.

My eyes were still black and blue, the swelling had gone down, but I was still self-conscious. He didn't push me for much or even demand sex, as he sometimes would. He kept hovering around me and wouldn't let me get my thoughts together. This weekend was filled with nothing but niceness and gifts. We later went to court and because I was uncooperative, the case was dropped. I was angry. Angry at him and myself, but I didn't want to testify about what had happened. I was ashamed and embarrassed and didn't want to relive it. It was bad enough I was having nightmares about it. After the case was dropped, I told him I was done. That he was as dead to me as our dead babies. This hurt him, he never forgave me for saying that to him.

Yet, he was still married and had his first child with his wife and baby number four total. Now she was pregnant again with number five. She got to keep her babies, but I couldn't keep mine. He said he needed me and my home so he would give me $5000 to stay, now I knew he was not serious. Although he was allegedly one of the top kingpins in the city and had money to spare, I knew he wasn't going to give me that kind of money. I figured I would call his bluff and be free. So I said no, make it $10,000 and we have a deal. And wouldn't you know this dude agreed? This was the day I made a deal with the devil. The love of money is the root of all evil. He gave me $5,000 upfront and then $1,000 every month for the next six. Yes, I said six, he threw an extra one in there just because. Now for a 21-year-old, that was a lot of money back then.

He promised to never put his hands on me like that again. And for a while, he held true to that. He never beat me again that bad, but in the end, they were pretty bad. However, he also knew he didn't have to. If he raised his voice, I would get skittish. One day, he came over and was fussing and I was curling my hair in the bathroom and had my 9mm on the counter. He laughed and asked what that was for? I said for you, I thought I needed to protect myself. He said, "If you pull it, then you better kill me or I'll kill you," and he walked off laughing.

He had broken me and he knew it. He would continue tearing me down now because he could. A few weeks after that, we were laying in bed and I got up to do something on the computer. He started fussing and had put some bass in his voice. I'm arguing back and run downstairs and get a knife. I go back in the room and he grabs me and all I know is I start slicing at his hands. I almost had cut off the tip of his thumb and two other fingers. Blood was everywhere. He is like why did you do that? I thought he was trying to fight me. The next thing he says is he is getting weak. I told him to go to the ER. He didn't think he could drive and was getting light-headed, so I had to take him. He gets dressed and wraps his hand in a towel. I am fussing the entire time, feeling relieved and somewhat powerful.

I dared him to try and get me arrested by saying I did it. I told him if he did, I would cut myself and say it was self-defense. After all, he was the criminal in this situation. He told the hospital staff that he was trying to break up a fight at the club and ended up needing stitches in two fingers. The thumb was the worst. He would never fully regain feeling in the tip of his thumb. I was expecting retribution, but he never did anything back for that. At least, not right away. I still paid for it. After this, he became more controlling. I fell in line, but I would rebel in my own ways. During this time, I had become more regular in church and I would ask the Lord for guidance, however, I was only hearing what I wanted to hear. I never would get a peace about either answer. Honestly, I don't think I wanted one.

I was so caught up in the tug-of-war and proving I was the better option. Hell, I had had him first. One day as we were talking, I asked him why he married her? He told me he would have married me first, but that I didn't need him and I was still trying to do my own thing. He knew he could trust her and she wouldn't leave, so he picked her. How true that was, I didn't know. It hurt though. He asked me what I wanted? I said I should be first. The things we say. I was truly young and dumb. They say be careful what you ask for. I didn't even see that he loved her. I think in his way, he loved us both and didn't know what to do with that.

In September of that year, he paid for a cruise for us. I kept telling myself it would be a defining moment for our relationship. I will never forget how excited and nervous I was. Not even two weeks before, the United States had been attacked and the World Trade Center Twin Towers destroyed, the Pentagon was damaged and another plane crashed all on the same day, on September 11th. I was packing the night before we were to drive to the airport in Birmingham. He had come over and we were talking while I was packing. I joked about how much I was carrying, but he was like I got it, you know I'll carry bags. He said he had a few errands to run, he would go home, get his bags, and be back. He left some money and the tickets. He said he wanted to leave it. He had too much cash on him. I didn't think anything about it.

We were leaving at 5:00 am and our flight was at 6:45 am, so at 4:30 am, I woke up and realized I hadn't heard from him. I called and called, to no avail. I'm waiting thinking to myself that he will be here. He doesn't show and it's now 5:15. I drag the bags to the car and start driving. At this point, all I could think is maybe he will meet me there, and that he is simply running late. Then I started wondering if something happened. In my heart, I knew that he was ok, it was something else. I called his house, Gina answered. I said hey, I need to know if he is there can I speak to him. She said he was and gave him the phone, he hung up on me. I cried all the way to Birmingham.

In disbelief and utter shock, I kept driving not even sure I was now going to make it. I couldn't believe he stood me up. I get to the airport and it is virtually empty. It's 6:15, I still have to park and get to the counter with my bags. This is before all the new protocols would be in place to better protect people. I park and get my bags out. I had three bags and they were loaded down. I was expecting help to carry them. I could barely carry all three, but I loaded myself down and took off for the counter. I could barely walk. I was all but dragging the bags. Tears were pouring down my face and no one was around. It was the longest walk of my life. As I finally cross the bridge and finally get to the entrance for the terminal I see a cart machine. I saw the machine, crossed the bridge, and dropped the bags. I couldn't make it any further. I ran to the machine, put my money in, and got a cart. I ran it back to my bags, loaded them up, and took off for the counter.

I have never seen an airport so empty in all my life. I made it to the counter right at 6:30. I ran up and asked if I was too late? The ticket agent looked at me with tears in my eyes and worked her magic. I have never been checked in so fast. She got me in, told me where to go, and said that I had just made it. I ran through the line to security and up to the gate. I still wasn't sure about the trip. I called Harmony and she got me together. She told me I was the strongest and bravest person she knew and this was a fully paid for trip. I better go and have a good time and don't worry about him until I get back. Say a prayer, be aware and I know your faith will bring you back home...I thanked her, dried my tears, and heard them call for me to board. I was flying first class for the first time and tried to enjoy the moment. I made the cruise and while I was still sad, I tried to make the best of the trip. I made peace and was ready to get back home.

However, I wouldn't be all the way back home from Birmingham before Cass started calling. I pulled up at the house and he is there waiting for me. I was livid at how nonchalant he was like I was coming from the store and he didn't stand me up. I wouldn't talk to him for two days but that didn't deter him. On that second day, he forced himself on me. He was tired of my attitude and wanted satisfaction. I fought him as hard as I could, but I lost that battle that night. I had developed a knack for going somewhere else in my mind while having sex. It would continue to help me for years. This wasn't the first time, nor would it be the last time, I would be forced to please him. My body would no longer belong to me. He only had to threaten me and I would give in. it wasn't worth the fight. It would be easier to give in and get it over with. He would remind me of our deal and I would at times feel like a slave. The more things got better, the more they stayed the same.

At 23, I had moved again to another home and had graduated college while working full-time. I had a chance to buy the house I was previously renting, but seeing as how I got persuaded to put my name on a house for his mother, I didn't think I would be able to buy the home and so I had to move. During this time, I was still seeing other guys whenever I could get moments away. I learned to be careful. It wasn't anything to have stolen moments with old friends every so often. One Saturday, while we were taking a nap, all of a sudden I hear someone yelling and kicking on my garage door. It's a female so I go to get my guns, while he tells me to stay inside he will go. Instead of going out of the garage, he goes out the front door. I grab a gun and follow. It's Gina, his wife, in the tricked out truck with my name on it. They are arguing. In the truck is her cousin with her child and Gina has brought their two kids with her. What is she thinking? She fusses about him being here and then she sees my gun and starts freaking out, asking, "Why do you have a gun? Are you crazy? I have my kids here." Ummm, lady are you crazy? You have come to my house kicking and screaming in my garage and you brought your kids here, no chick you are obviously the crazy one." So while they are fussing, I go right in the truck and grab the keys before anyone can say anything.

This was crazy because when I got the truck, he wouldn't even let me use it when I wanted to. One night, after we got into it about something, I went and got the truck and hid it from him. I told him if I couldn't drive it, she couldn't drive it unless he was in it. If I ever saw her in it, I would take it. Yeah, I know I was being petty, but I didn't care. I exerted what little power I had when I could. I always kept my own key for anything that my name was on. So for her to have driven the truck over here and not her Acura was a violation. And she was not going to be driving that truck anywhere else. So she asks me for the key and I have a few choice words for her. She is now telling him to make me give her the key and he looks at me. If looks could kill, they would all be dead. He looked at me. She was like well rig it and he was like hell no.

All of a sudden, the police are pulling up. Not surprised by the neighborhood I lived in, which was mostly white upper-middle class. And here you have these black people yelling and acting a fool in the driveway. The officer comes up to assess the situation. He asks about the pistol in my hand and if I have a permit. I say yes and go get it. He asks why I have it? I explained that this is my house and that she came over yelling, screaming, and banging on my garage like a madwoman. She says she wants to go home, but I won't give the key back to the truck. I then explained that the truck and the insurance is in my name, and it will be over my dead body before she drives that truck home.

I told the officer that technically she stole the truck. I don't care if they call a cab or pile up in his Honda, but that truck is not moving. He asks that I go and put the gun up back in the house before we continue talking. I do. When I come back out, he asks if he can talk to me and Cass inside? He again asks about the key to the truck. I again say no. He and the officer are talking about how to get them all home, while also going back and forth, talking to Gina. It has now been two hours and I am tired and angry. I ask Cass how she even got the key to drive the truck? He says he left them hanging on a key ring, and she must have taken them. They all can't fit in the Honda and a cab is out of the question. They didn't want to call anybody else. I tell the officer I could care less, but all of them need to leave my house. Him, her, the cousin, everybody just leave.

The officer explains that legally he can not force me to do anything since the truck is mine and in my yard. However, to bring this to a close, he asked if I would let Cass drive them in the truck home? At this point, I say, "Cass drives the truck and she can drive his car because I don't want his car left here. I don't want to see or hear from anyone." Cass and Gina both agree. I go outside to be sure they are all out of my truck and in the car because I was not playing about her driving that truck. They all load up and leave. The officer leaves and I go inside and call my girl. This was a mess and I was outdone. Apparently so was Gina. I tried to leave Cass, but with a mortgage and a truck in my name that I knew I couldn't afford, I was stuck. I didn't even think that he would not let his truck get taken or his mom put out, I was worried about my credit rating. I knew that it would be months before either would be taken. Rather than call his bluff, I stayed. Trapped still. Not long after this, their relationship would spin out of control and she would leave him.

This would also be a period in my life when I would take over and become the director of the Nursery at church. Although I was at church every Sunday, I would miss out on most teachings because most Sundays I would end up working in the Nursery. It was ok. I loved the babies. However, this would eventually take a toll on my Spiritual life. Gina and Cass divorced, although I knew that he would not leave her completely alone. Besides the kids they had, I knew he would still sleep with her. I had grown to realize that he loved her and she loved him.

She needed him in a way I never did nor ever would, and somehow he needed that. Men want to feel loved, needed, and appreciated. However, it was still the same game only the positions changed. One night he took me out to his house, the house that they had shared, and said you should live here with me. His home was paid for. A 3000 square foot four-bedroom, three-bathroom home. It was nice, out in the country on three acres. Financially, it made sense, saved me money, especially now that we had started talking about marriage. We were practically living together at this point, but this was going to be official. I wasn't sure, but this is what I had been fighting for, for years. I had won, but it felt like I was losing. I wasn't even sure I wanted it anymore. We had already been together off and on for nine years. He hadn't put his hands on me in a year. It seemed to make sense that we should be together. I said I loved him. I thought I did. Looking back I loved him for what I thought love was then. Now I know it wasn't love. I got out of my lease a month early and moved in with him.

I would have nightmares and demonic dreams almost the entire time I lived there about that house. I wouldn't even realize it for years and not until I moved out of the house. My mother was not keen on the idea of us living together, but as I told her, "You are not keen on it because it gives the illusion of immorality. But that is because you and everyone else is assuming that we are sleeping together, although you don't know we are sleeping together. You assume we are. Well, are you assuming that every person who is dating someone is sleeping together? We have sex now, so you are telling me it's worse that we live together." Oh, we went round and round and in the end, I still did it. I didn't even have a ring.

There was no fanfare or romantic engagement. We talked about it and said we were going to do it and I kept wearing a ring that he had given me the money to buy a year earlier. Just a ring that I had liked not an official engagement ring. I said I didn't need all that. Now I know that I want all of that. Looking back, that was a hard time for him. I began to see the chinks in his armor.

Things changed almost immediately when I moved in. There were pictures on the wall of Gina and the kids. I took them down and he put them back up. I asked why? He said his kids were in the picture. I said, "Well, put them somewhere else." He said, "I put them where I want them, and you better not touch them again. You are here she is not. You got me, so you should not let a picture bother you, but you heard what I said." I knew by his tone he was serious and I would not argue with it. It was also during this time that he started becoming even more controlling. The once laid back guy that I knew, when it came to matters of the house, was now extremely picky. He said that was my house so he didn't care, but this was his house and he cared. He took care of the yard and outside work and I took care of the inside. Sometimes he would help.

He washed clothes and ironed. I needed to fold and put them up. Since he paid for the house, he would pay the utility bill, but since he was hardly there, it was on me to pay for the phone, cable, and internet. The truck was finally paid off. But now I had two more loans in my name. Sometime after I moved in, I had talked to my pastor and explained my new living situation. I didn't want to be a hypocrite and I knew the church's stance on a man and woman living together. As my pastor stated the appearance of evil, it was what it was. He didn't condemn me or make me feel bad. He said that although we were engaged, but not married, he would need me to step down until I was married. I respected that and he even offered to do a ceremony in his office ahead of the big wedding we were planning. I went to Cass and I asked him what he wanted to do? I told him I didn't want to force anything I didn't think we were ready for. I honestly would have stepped down from the ministry and I told him that. He said he didn't have a problem with it and so we started counseling. We were honest to an extent.

We didn't lie, we omitted some big things, such as his main profession, cheating, the physical and emotional abuse, his temper, and controlling ways. Cass was charismatic when he wanted to be. He was well-liked, smart, and he knew what to say. He was charming and knew the Bible well. Then there was his dark side. The murderous side. I once asked him had he killed anyone himself, and he said yea. I asked for details, but he wouldn't give them. I thought it best that I didn't know. My pastor thought we were a good fit for each other. In June, we got married one Sunday after church in his office. Our big wedding would be a year later almost to the day.

That would be the day we would celebrate as our official anniversary. He wasn't helping me pay my bills. Bills I incurred without him were my responsibility he said. He was now saying times were a little hard. I did what I always did. Work. I went out and got a part-time job in addition to my full-time job to help pay my bills. After we got married, he wanted to know my every move. I was literally stuck to my phone. He would call all day to "check on me" or ask irrelevant questions. Since we would sometimes not see each other and he would come home when I was gone, it would sometimes be a day or two before I saw him. If I didn't answer the phone, he would call until I did and then I would have a barrage of questions.

Everything wasn't all bad all the time. When we didn't have attitudes with each other, we got along as we did in the beginning. We laughed, acted silly, and talked a lot. He still told me most things. We would even talk about the other women and business. Around this time, Cass decided to make up for the cruise he stood me upon. He decided he wanted to go to Disneyworld. We both had never been and thought it would be fun. We decided to drive there. Outside of Birmingham, we get pulled over for speeding. The officer explains why he pulled us over and asks us where we are going? While running our information, Cass realizes he has the .38 pistol in his pocket and it is noticeable. We already have two other 9mm also in the car. As we debate how to play this out, he asks if I took all the guns out before we packed the car up. I said yes, that we should only have the ones we took from the house, which were all mine. He asks me about the one under my seat and oops, I realize there is an extra one. We can't remember if it's mine or not.

However, we decided it best to alert the officer since I have my permit with me. When the officer comes back, he proceeds to tell him that we have weapons on us. The officer asks us to get out of the car. He pulls the gun from Cass's pocket. He asks if we have a permit and I say yes. He then asks to search the vehicle for the other weapons. He finds the other guns. The officer is now asking me a million questions. I pull out our travel reservations and show him we are indeed going to Disneyworld. The officer asks if I am military, I say no. Am I CIA? No. FBI? No. A hitwoman? No. He says young lady why do you have so many weapons? I say because I am single and need to protect myself. He looks and says since we were honest and everything checks out, we are free to go but to put the guns unloaded in the trunk. We do and head on our way. Cass and I laugh about it the rest of the way. We surmised that the officer thought I was a Queen in the game and Cass was my driver/bodyguard. He heard Florida and assumed we were going for drugs. I had made runs before but this wasn't it. We were always more careful for those.

The trip was a great vacation. We had the best time. Moments like these made things seem worthwhile. At home, we were constantly eating out and hanging out. It was always VIP when we went out. Security making sure we had front door parking and the best tables in the house. Nobody stepped to Cass. Most were trying to join in the festivities, especially if he was paying. Everyone knew he was no one to be messed with. Cass was a fighter, and I never heard of a fight he lost. Cass also had many people loyal to him. People may not have liked him or even respected him, but most were afraid of him.

One day my phone died while at my aunt's house and I had left my charger at home. When I got home, he grabbed me by the throat until I showed him how the phone had died. He let me go and later made sure I had a charger I could keep on me. I was having doubts about going forward with the big wedding. I hadn't changed my name and didn't plan to change my name with the thought that if this doesn't work, I won't have to change my name back. Now, who thinks like that? If you are expecting your marriage to last, that alone was reason enough. A few months after our ceremony while working my part-time job, I would get into it with an associate. The situation had escalated over a few days culminating with her trying to run me off the road. For this, my patience had worn thin. I expected my husband to handle it, but he was calmer than I expected or liked.

One night I took it upon myself to confront her. I punch her and she pulls out a box cutter. I asked her why she brought a knife to a gunfight. I tell her to hold on and this stupid girl waits and watches me walk back to my car reach under my seat and pull out my pistol. Everyone is standing there watching me as I walk back up. As I get closer, I load one in the chamber and cock the gun. Now everyone is running. I run after her and the gun goes off. I ended up arrested and in jail, charged with a misdemeanor gun charge. I received probation for a year. I was off in six months, once I paid the fine. He was supposed to be there to handle the situation well, or at least be back up. I could handle her on my own, but he was late. I never understood why he was so laid back about it, especially, when if the roles were reversed, he would not have stopped until somebody's blood was pouring? I was so mad, I got caught. I was actually thinking of a job with the FBI, but now I had a criminal record so that was out.

Although I had a gun charge, you would think they would want someone who doesn't mind using a handgun. The crazy thing is, I had gotten my hair done, (had my weave touched up). Long, flowing curls, and I'm in a sweatshirt, jeans, and Timberland boots. I was cute in my mugshot. Thank God this was before everything was online. So no, you can not Google it. I remember calling and telling him you were late to the fight, but you better be about your business getting me out of here.

Those two hours felt like two weeks. I am not made for jail. I tell you what, I would've been in there handling it. Thank God for favor, grace, and mercy. Cass was mad I didn't wait. I was mad he was late. He thought it was the funniest thing ever. He didn't think I was a true fighter, but like I told him, everyone has limits. The truth of it was I had always been a fighter, my limits were a lot farther out. Over the years, they had gotten shorter. Let's say I learned a strong lesson on controlling my anger. I would be more calculated the next time the need would arise.

Time passed and our upcoming nuptials were fast approaching. Our wedding almost went off without a hitch. I would give him his family invitations to pass out, but he got too busy to do so and although they knew about it, they were offended they didn't get the invitation. Most didn't show up. It was still a beautiful day. His family had an attitude and they blamed me. Not a good start too the family. All my family came. I was so surprised. I didn't think they would, but I was so touched they did. A month after the wedding, Cass and I got into it over something and as I was trying to leave and pull off, he ended up taking a bat to the back window on the driver's side of my car. He said he wasn't trying to, but if you weren't trying to, then you wouldn't have swung it. All of this over a misunderstanding.

Within a couple of hours, he already had another one ordered. Craziness. The only time I could not answer the phone immediately was when I was at work. Trust, he was calling my desk phone and my cell. And there was a time limit for me to call back. If I was in a long meeting, then I would have to leave the meeting and call back to tell him I was in a long meeting. This was before texting took over and it became the standard for communication. During this time, he also would go to church with me sometimes. He could quote the Bible better than I could. He would reference that he knew God had been on His side more than once. He didn't believe he needed to go to church all the time for his relationship with God. However, he was fine with me going to church.

It had also come out that while I knew he was sleeping with his ex, he was now sleeping with at least two more. I knew he was a cheater. I was surprised at the abundance of cheating that he was doing, but not that he was cheating. See I married him knowing he was a cheater. He had cheated with me for years and I went into it knowing that he would cheat on me. How mad could I be at something I knew? This is one of the things we didn't talk about before marriage. One of the few stipulations we talked about was that he was not to come home with any diseases or children. I didn't like it, we even talked about it, but he said that we were fine. Our sex life was ok.

The fact that I knew when he was going to be sleeping with someone else, didn't necessarily keep me longing to sleep with him. It turned me off from him. He was not one to let me out of my "wifely" duties regardless of what time it was when he would come home. I would later realize that years of Depo and pills would also help contribute to my diminished sex drive. One of his phones was in my name and Sprint was one of the first companies to allow you to go online to see text messages and GPS tracking.

My oh my...every night and throughout the day, I was checking to see where he was. I knew where all his other girls stayed and doing some backtracking was even able to get names and phone numbers. I could easily be a detective when I wanted. One night he was at his ex's house. I had called him. He lied and said he was working. I had called him earlier and he was supposed to have been home for a dat e and for some loving. He canceled the date but said he would get home to take care of his husbandly duties. So here he was with her and not me and this was one of the few times I called to say I wanted him. Oh no, this did not go over well with me. Honey, let me tell you, I felt tonight was a good night for payback. I grabbed my gun, threw it in my back waistband, and headed out.

She only lived six minutes away. I went to her house, rang that doorbell, and said she needed to send my husband out. He was right behind her at the door since it was 1:00 am. She told him to handle this and went back inside. He asked what I was doing here. I said, "Hell, what are you doing here? Your kids are asleep and this is not your home or work. This is not working and you need to be getting to the house before or soon after me. Don't stand me up to come over here. You should have taken care of me first, then brought your sorry tail here." I stood at the door and waited for him to put his clothes back on and come out that door. Lord, I tell you what.

He had parked his car down the street since she lived next door to her parents and her mother couldn't stand him. I had parked right next to him, so there we were walking down the road together. He looked at me and shook his head. He said, "Shari, I don't understand you sometimes." I said, "I never do you, but either way you don't need to come back here tonight." He went home, changed his clothes. I honestly can't remember if we had sex or not. But I know he went out to the studio for a while and then he was gone by the time I woke up in the morning. I figured he was gone before daybreak. I didn't even care. I was determined to win as many little battles as I could. And that was a win.

My next win would come when I would cuss him out for missing a flight to NY for a showcase because he was with one of his girls. The showcase was a success and a few major and minor record companies were interested in him, but he would not follow through on that path. Since he had a state-of-the-art studio, he wanted a distribution deal instead of a record deal. He was one of the best to come from Huntsville, but as I told him you are still an unknown. There wasn't anything he couldn't do with his hands. Cass was a regular mister: fix it, build it, paint it. You name it, he could do it. And he was a smart man. Very good with numbers. However, the call of the streets was too strong.

On the outside, things looked good, but on the inside, stress fractures had been happening for years. And it was all about to come to a head. Cass could be mean and demeaning. One night, he got mad at me and he got on the phone with one of his girls while sitting and looking at me. I looked at him and said am I supposed to be concerned about you talking to one of your chicks in front of me? Does she know she is not the only one? He hurried up and got off that phone. Touche. I said as he got up and did something in the back and then left.

THE DOOR

The night before his 30th birthday, I hadn't seen him much. He had been in and out all day. The last time he left, I knew he was going to see his ex. I didn't say anything and I wasn't worried about it. I waited for a while, tried calling him right at midnight, but he didn't answer. I went to bed. Around six I woke up and checked to see if he was home he wasn't and he wasn't in the studio. He had come back though. The clothes he had on when I last saw him was in a pile on the floor. So he had come home and left back out. I was about to lay down when Gina called me. She said, "Cass has been shot and I think you should get to the hospital ASAP." I asked, "What? By who? What happened?" She said, "Shari get to the hospital. All I know is my mom shot him and it's not looking good, so you need to go." Then she hung up. I rushed and put clothes on and raced to the hospital. I got there and all they told me was that he was in critical condition and in surgery.

While I waited, the police came to talk to me. They asked me when was the last time I had seen him and what his relationship was to his ex-mother-in-law and his ex-wife? They explained to me that she shot him three times in the back. A difference of opinions arose and an argument happened. He was trying to leave when she shot him three times in the back. He stumbled to his truck and tried to drive away, but he was losing so much blood, he crashed into a ditch. She had called 911 and when the ambulance arrived, he had stumbled out of the truck. He was so critical, they called a med-flight to get him to the hospital. They did not expect him to survive.

He was in ICU for a week with tubes everywhere. He was in the hospital for another couple of days, before he would be able to come back home.

I was humiliated, not to mention one of his girlfriends had her husband bring her to the hospital to see him. She was lucky I was still on probation, otherwise I would have put her in ICU next to him. I could've gone back there and pulled out every tube in him. I grabbed her with her tears in her eyes and asked her what she was doing here? She had said she knew something was wrong with him and she had to see him. I said, "Girl, you real bold and if I wasn't on probation I would drag you through this hospital." I let her see him, but I didn't let her stay. On top of all of that, all of this was playing out in the news. I never thought he would go that far. The grand jury wouldn't know whose story to believe, so no charges would be filed against either one of them.

He wasn't home one day before I was getting ready for work and he was on the phone with the same married side chick. I said to him, " You almost died. I am here changing your bandages and you can't even wait till I go to work?" He said, "I didn't hear right." He made a miraculous recovery. In another week, he was up and moving around better. Almost a month later on my birthday, I called him to confirm our plans. He wasn't answering. I had a feeling and I checked GPS. He was at his homeboy's house. However, something wasn't right. I rode out there and I saw Gina's car. I ring the doorbell and he opens the door. She is behind him with a stained face like she has been crying. He asks me to leave because he needs to talk to her. I said she is crazy and her mama is crazy and one of them is going to kill you. I told him don't worry about me. I was done. I left and went straight to the U-haul place to try and rent a U-haul for that evening. They were all rented out.

However, I would not be deterred. I went back to work and asked my sister-friend to meet me at my house after work with her truck. Called my other sister and asked her to meet me at the house after work with her truck as well. She brought my mother along. I told them I was tired of his crap and I was leaving. Let's pack up and take as much as we can. My mom tried to hug me and I got short with her. I told her don't, I don't need a hug. I was on a mission. I wanted to do this as quickly as possible before he got home. I hadn't been answering his calls. Of course, he comes home while we are packing up. He speaks and looks. He goes to the back to get something and then leaves again. He calls me to ask if I am leaving. I say, "Yes." He is like why? You don't have to leave. I told him I can't, it has been too much.

I tell him I can't get everything and I'll be back for the rest once I figure it all out. We take as much as we can. I know him to like to set fire to things and throw things away, so I was trying to be sure I got most of my clothes and certain things that meant the most to me. I moved back in with my parents. I had nowhere else to go and I needed time to figure out what I was going to do. I should have been relieved, but I was mad. Then I was sad. The whole time I was lost. I didn't tell anybody I had left him. The first couple of days were pretty quiet. I went a few days later to get a few more things. I would try to go when I thought he wouldn't be home. After a week, he was asking when I was coming home. I told him I didn't know. Every time I thought about it, I would go to the house and some chick would be there. Once it was the ex, twice it was the married chick, and once was the young chick. During this time, I wasn't sure if I would be able to support myself. I had two jobs, but we also had accumulated quite a few bills together.

Sometimes, he would threaten to not pay or would give me the money late. At times, he would get irrational and threaten me and my family if I didn't come back or if I didn't want to see him. One night while I was out with some friends, he was in a mood and wanted to see me. I didn't want to, but he insisted. I took longer than he liked and once again, I was choked and punched in my back. He wanted some head and he wanted it from me. Tonight he would be stubborn and intoxicated on something and would slap me in my face for taking too long and not doing it right. I suggested that we have sex, but he did not want that. He finally was able to cum and I was free to go home. This was more about power than sexual satisfaction. In his mind, this was only temporary. I couldn't even see the blessings that God was trying to do for me. It had been eight months now. He had grown tired of me being gone.

I had stepped out and found an apartment I liked. I was scared I wouldn't be able to afford it. I didn't even think I would get approved, but I did. Fear would have me turn it down. Fear of being able to support myself, fear of retribution from him, and ultimately, fear of him. Like I said I knew he was a cheater when I married him, so this wasn't something I didn't know and I wanted to say it was a problem. Now after 10+ years, I knew who I married and maybe this was as good as it was going to get for me. I was still broken. I hadn't dealt with being molested and raped as a child. I hadn't dealt with my depression, low self-esteem, or drinking. I was ashamed that I had allowed my life to come to this. But this had been the only man to want to be with me and fight to be with me. For all the bad, this is what I thought love would look like for me. I can't lie there were good times between us and benefits to being with him. On good days we would laugh and be silly together, talk about the things we wanted and trips we would take. So in the ninth month, I decided to go back. He had gotten tired and the threats were happening more often.

He would later say that he didn't threaten me to come back and that I could have left since he was wrong and he would have been ok with that. I always have to remind him his version was not the reality of the situation. He will admit that he was tired of how things were and wanted me back. I never understood why. I never thought he would not let me go. Two words, power, and control. I wasn't home a good month before I regretted my decision. I knew I had made a mistake. We weren't the same and I was ready for something better. Before I could get together to leave again, I found out I was pregnant. I was so upset. I had recently got accepted into an MBA program and I had decided I didn't want kids at all. I didn't want to be tied to him. How did this happen?

Well, I knew I wasn't leaving now. I knew I was going to be moody and he deserved to put up with me. I was so upset when I found out. My sister was so excited and laughed at me. I cussed her out at that nail shop. I considered having an abortion. I told God there would be only one way I wouldn't end up back at that clinic and if this was twins. I went to the doctor and they thought I was trying to miscarry. She sent me for an ultrasound and let me tell you what, there were two fertilized eggs in there, but they didn't want to say I was having twins or even one child. I was barely four weeks and hearts don't start beating until six.

I would have to come back in a week and a half to confirm the pregnancy. They thought my body would absorb or miscarry one or both. I knew that neither of those would happen. This was God answering my prayer. The cramping immediately stopped and when I went back, I had two heartbeats. From that moment, I knew it would be what I had asked God for. A boy and a girl and my boy would be born first. I would say this throughout my entire pregnancy. Cass was excited to have finally gotten me pregnant. He loved kids and I will say he is a good father to his kids. Not a good husband or boyfriend, but he has never abused kids. Now, I was going to be a mother.

A few months into the pregnancy, my phone died and I had to use one of his while I waited for my new one to come. On it, were videos of him with some chick in Atlanta. They were in bed together. I was so done. I called him and told him and he didn't even seem to care. I told him he couldn't be stressing me out like this and I was tired and completely over it. I was eerily calm. I told him I was done caring. He brushed me off for the most part. That was the moment when I knew I had fallen out of love with him. I was done, but I was gonna stay. With two babies on the way, I didn't know how I would make it on my own. I had resigned myself to the fact that this was going to be life. Hey, other people live like this. I didn't hate him. I still cared about him.

A few months later, I would ask to go on a short trip to Nashville or somewhere. He always was putting me off. I would later find pictures of him and another chick he took to Nashville. He told me he was working with his homeboy on his cd release launch and party. He had called me to check to see if he had left something in the truck, instead I found the pictures from Rock City. I had been accustomed to checking that little compartment in the trunk. That was where he would hide condoms, lubricants, pictures, and drugs. We weren't using condoms, but I was at least glad to know he was. I wasn't upset about the girl. I was upset he took her and still hadn't taken me anywhere. When he came home, I gave him the pictures and said, "Well, I'm glad you were able to have a getaway and walked off." I didn't even want to talk about it. He gave me some excuse, but I told him to stop. It didn't matter. We still portrayed the happy couple but we were only going through the motions for the most part. Don't get me wrong, there were happy times in there, times we would laugh and be silly and we still talked, but that love wasn't there. I don't know, maybe I was looking for what I read about in the fairytales.

I wanted peace and true happiness. Well, real joy. I had worked up until three weeks before the twins actually came. The doctor had ordered me off work and to rest more. My body was retaining fluid and most of it was in my legs. We were sure they were coming early, but we would have to go in and get them. Around 33 weeks, I was having to go up to the hospital once a week to have stress tests to see how the twins were doing. Basically, I lay in a bed, they strap this device to my belly to monitor their heartbeats for about 30 minutes, and then I could go home. As we moved into 36 weeks, I was having to go twice a week.

My doctor was going to be going on vacation for a week going into my 38th week. We wanted to induce at 36.5 weeks. The high-risk doctor that would have had to sign off on it, said no since the babies were seemingly fine. Although she was concerned about the fluid I was retaining, it still wasn't enough for him. So I waited. Well, I thought I had made it. Friday I was on my way for my stress test. I was going to go up here then go get some lunch and maybe do some last-minute shopping. I was excited because I had made it. My doctor would be back Sunday. I'm strapped in doing fine. Usually, the nurse does everything and I leave, but here walks in a doctor.

She was concerned about the swelling in my legs. The doctor on call was concerned and so they started running some tests. The babies were fine, but I was now showing signs of preeclampsia, pregnancy-induced high blood pressure. They said my legs had swollen as much as they could and if I retained any more fluid, they would start tearing and bleeding. I tried everything to get them to let me go home and stay on bed rest. I wanted to wait for my doctor. We had grown so close, she had given me her cell number to call her if I did go into labor. Of course, I called and of course, she agreed and told me to stay and let them induce me. Well alrighty then. I had a birth plan I had submitted weeks ago and she assured me the on-call doctor, Dr. L was good.

I made all the necessary calls to my husband and my mom. I had the bags packed. I needed him to bring them. I was glad I had done that a few days prior. So on a Friday at 1:00 pm, my labor was induced. I was anxious and excited to finally meet these little humans that had taken up residence inside my body. I was ready to get my body back, to sleep more peacefully, and be rid of this heartburn. Now it was a waiting game. I had Cass sneak me some food up around 7:00 pm because I was starving. My mom and sister had come with great anticipation. Everyone else we said we would call when it got closer to push time. I determined I would not be having an epidural. My back already hurt and I didn't want any more complications. I only took the pain meds they could put in the IV. I was informed they could only give them to me up until I was 7cm.

After that, I was on my own to get to 10 and to push so that it wouldn't affect the twins and delivery. This was ok by me, I had developed a high tolerance for pain dealing with asthma and in and out of hospitals. Friday night was long and slow. With the limited channels, somehow I got stuck watching a channel that was playing a marathon of Fresh Prince of Bel-Air. After about four hours, I was tired of hearing the opening song. I was like please shut that darn tv off. Every couple of hours, a nurse was coming in, checking me. Saturday morning I was only like 2 or 3cm. Cass had already left a few hours ago. I told him we would call him when it got close. I told my mom and sister to leave. Mom didn't want to go, but like I told her, I had a long time to go and when I get close it will be plenty of time for them to make it.

Saturday, I was actually able to get some better rest. Pain was bearable, my menstrual cramps were a little worse than these contractions. By Saturday night, I was only five cm. The contractions were beginning to take their toll and the meds weren't helping as much. I was sore and that was causing me pain. I had a hard time getting comfortable and of course, I wasn't going to get any good rest. My mom and LT and Cass had all come back during the day and then I sent them all off again. Saturday goes and still no babies. Sunday morning, my mom and LT, and Cass are back again. They are the only ones I would let come up.

Dr. L comes in, I am only at 6.5 cm. They had already given me meds to try and help progress my labor, but nothing was helping. He had received my full chart and was aware that due to some scar tissue I had from a LEEP procedure years earlier for a cancer scare it was affecting my uterus being able to contract as it needed to. The babies were fine, but he was concerned about my health as my levels were dropping. He had come into the room and was facing my mom and sister on the couch talking to them. I sat up and said why are you talking to them, they can not make a decision for me. You need to talk to me. (I was tired, hungry, thirsty, and over this labor).

He told me if he would have known this, then he would not have let me go this long. And my option was to try and continue to deliver vaginally or go ahead and have a C-section. He did not recommend me continuing with a vaginal birth, due to the length of time I had been in labor and the fact that they couldn't determine how much longer it would take me to get to 10 cm. I looked at him and asked what he would recommend if I was his daughter and he said a c-section. And so a c-section I was going to have. He left to have the OR prepared and my doctor called. She was calling to check on me and thought I had had the babies.

I explained to her what was decided. She agreed and was a little upset they hadn't seen the note about my scar tissue earlier and had let me go so long. She was back, but she told me Dr. L was a good surgeon and I was in good hands. When he came back, he informed me that my white blood count was dangerously low along with other levels, and at this point, I could no longer get an epidural for the c-section because they were afraid I would bleed out. So I needed full anesthesia. He also said that his plan would be to continue with the plan of a tubal ligation unless circumstances would prevent that. This however meant they only had eight minutes to get the babies out before it would affect them. This is what they do, so off we go. I would not be awake for the delivery, so I promised Cass that no matter what, make sure the babies were good, and to stay with them and not worry about me. I had lived an ok life, my babies deserved to live theirs. Ironic how nine months ago, I was ready to end a life again, but now after carrying them and feeling life inside of me, it became all about them. As a mother, I would lay down my life, if it meant they could live.

At all costs, they were to save the babies over me. I remember laying on the table and counting back from 10. I think I got to eight barely before I was out. I would awake to them shaking me in recovery and telling me to breathe. I remember thinking I am breathing crazy people. What are you talking about? It took a minute for my vision to come back and everyone seemed a little more antsy than normal. It did seem a little hard to breathe, but coming out of anesthesia and surgery I was foggy. I finally came around enough for them to explain that I had exasperated on the table. (I threw up in the tube they had put in my throat that was breathing for me. It got into my lungs, which they had to suction out and it caused me to have double pneumonia).

The doctor was still able to deliver a healthy baby boy at 12:26 weighing four pounds and 11 ounces and 18 inches long and a healthy baby girl at 12:27 pm weighing six pounds and five ounces on a beautiful Sunday, almost 48 hours to the mark from when I was induced. He was also able to do my tubal ligation. I however was on my way to ICU, so they could get better control of my breathing and apparently my bleeding. As I was being wheeled to the back elevator to go up to ICU, they were able to bring the babies by so I could see them. However, it was brief since this was out of the baby safe zone and the alarms had started going off. I was able to see them and give them a quick kiss before the nurses were running back to the nursery. I was in ICU with oxygen on my face and a morphine pump hooked up to my IV. I was still out of it. Cass had come up to check on me, but then I remember alarms going off and nurses running into my room. Dr. L came in and all I got was that I was bleeding a lot into my abdomen. It was pooling and so he was going to push on my already tender, got cut open and sewn back together belly to push the blood out.

He said it would hurt. He pushed and I yelled and hit the morphine pump and I believed I passed out from the pain. I can't even tell you where the blood came out of or where it went. Cass had literally ran up out of the room I am told. I would later be told that I almost died again and that I had lost so much blood they would call for blood from the pharmacy. I don't remember much after the push. I remember waking up and it was Monday. Don't remember much about that day at all. I do remember a pushy nurse asking me about breast-feeding and what I wanted them to do about the babies.

I was like well ma'am I hope you have fed my babies some formula while waiting on me. She said they had, but asked if I wanted to start pumping. Although the milk couldn't be used because of the meds I was on, it could help with my flow. I was in no form to even try to pump, but I took it anyway. I vaguely remember family coming to see me. I become more coherent on Tuesday. I remember my godmother GG coming to see me. I hadn't seen the babies yet and she said she was going to break me out of there to see the babies if they wouldn't let me go.

After begging and promising to keep the oxygen mask on and not get out of the wheelchair, I could go. And away we went. I got down there and they were the only babies in the nursery. They were running some tests on Prince so she gave me Princess first. She was this little round chubby thing. She was still small though. The cutest thing I had ever seen and she was mine. I got a few minutes with her and was able to feed her and then I held and fed this little skinny boy of mine. He was long and skinny. I guess Princess was eating more when in the womb, but he was healthy although he had a touch of jaundice. I was only down there for probably 30 minutes. I remember kissing them, telling them I loved them, and back I was headed to ICU.

Cass finally came back to see me. I asked him what took him so long? He said my instructions to him were to make sure the babies were good and that's what he was doing. And he didn't prefer to see me like this. I guess he preferred either alive or dead, he didn't do the in-between. I stayed in ICU until Wednesday evening. I was moved back down to the labor and delivery floor in a regular room. They would bring the babies to see me, but since they were the only ones in the nursery they didn't have to stay overnight because they were getting all the attention anyway. Nurses were spoiling the babies from day 1.

I was told that they thought about sending the babies home without me, but since the nursery was empty they got to stay and wait on me. My doctor came to see me and we discussed this eventful birth. She explained to me that I had helped her faith by my constant faith. I had said from day one, I would have a boy and a girl and my boy would be first and I even knew who was who. I never faltered or wavered. I explained my talk with God and His confirmation. Since this was the only thing I had talked to him about, I knew he would honor my request. I was so blessed by that and that my faith helped increase someone else's.

On Friday, we all went home. I knew that I would be doing a lot by myself with the way Cass stayed on the go. My mom stayed the first night, but having stayed a week in the hospital I was able to maneuver a bit better. Still moving slowly, but better. My mom and sister would take turns that first week coming out and checking on me and helping with the twins. I wouldn't let anyone hold them long after they were asleep. My thought was while they were small and I could hold them both it was fine, but when they got bigger, who was going to be able to hold two sleeping babies. No sir no ma'am. The twins came home eating every 3-4 hours. I guess having to share they didn't require as much and held it longer, I don't know. I know I did pray that they liked to sleep and would be on a schedule early because I would need all the help I could get. And guess what that prayer was answered too! I tried to breastfeed, but they couldn't latch that well and my milk never came in.

I managed to barely pump a full 8 oz every day. They got 4 - 6 oz of breast milk every day. After about four weeks, I stopped because I was barely able to get them that. That's ok, the formula was fine with me. We had to go to a soy formula because Princess would spit up a lot. Had to run tests and found out she had reflux pretty bad. Had to stop her halfway through and burp her and be sure she was pretty upright when she ate. After the first month, Prince had plumped up and was the bigger of the two, and he has since stayed that way. We got into a good routine, and at six weeks, they were sleeping through the night! Yes, God! I stayed home for eight weeks with the twins.

My mom thought she would be able to keep them when I went back to work, I knew better. Three days a week they went to daycare and she would keep them Tuesday and Thursday. She was glad I did that once she started keeping them. She watched them for a few months until they were a little bigger and older and then they went to daycare full-time. During this time, Cass was gone for most late-night feedings. He would come home and try to see them before bedtime. Usually, he was in and out. And Princess was a daddy's girl since in my belly. He would try to be sure to be home to help me feed and dress them for school and so I could get to work. Like I said, I had a routine and they were on the same schedule. They ate, slept, and even pooped at the same time. Prince was usually the first up, so I would be able to get a few minutes with him, and then by the time I was ready for Princess if she wasn't awake, I had to wake her up.

They would sleep together so if you moved one, it wouldn't be long before the other awakened. I don't care how far apart you put them, they would find each other and sleep under each other. It wasn't until they started rolling that they slept in separate cribs. I was in the role of mommy and not that concerned any longer with the comings and goings of Cass. I knew I would be doing a lot by myself and I was ok with that. I had a routine, but it was better when we worked together and he was home to help, especially as they got older and bigger. When the twins were six months, I turned 30. No real fanfare, but I was glad to have made it. I marveled at how I had been blessed to be alive and be a mom.

THE WINDOW

Two months to the day after my birthday, February 15th, I awoke to being punched in my face. I was drug out of bed and beaten savagely. He grabbed a gun and put it to my head. Prince had woken up and was crying. I ran and grabbed him. He told me to put him down so he could kill me. I prayed to God, but I wouldn't put my son down. I told him he would have to do it with him in my arms. Cass was a wreck I had never seen him cry nor that angry. He had come home and checked my phone and saw text messages between me and a guy that I was secretly seeing. We hadn't seen each other much since the birth of the twins, but we talked pretty regularly. I usually erased all our messages and I swore I did before I went to bed, but I guess I didn't. Cass was heartbroken. He said he never expected me to cheat on him. I always said if I had to cheat I would leave.

I don't know why I didn't leave. I should have left when he was dead wrong but this is now my fault. Ironically, he was still cheating on me, but my deception was the ultimate betrayal and a major blow to his ego. He could not handle it. With a gun to my head, he slumped on the floor and we all cried. He got up, looked at me, and with evil in his eyes had never seen before he said, I am not going to kill you because I don't have the time to stop and raise these kids like they need to be, nor find someone to do it in a short time and your parents are old and retired. So for these kids, I'll let you live. He went and put the gun up, came back and snatched Prince out of my arms, and laid him back in his crib. He dragged me down the hall to the other bedroom and told me to take my clothes off. He took his clothes off and told me to get in the bed. I was so afraid I obliged. Still not knowing if he was going to kill me or not.

He said I am still his wife and he suggests I please him like my life depended on it. When it was over, we laid there. I was up all night. In the morning around six, he called my mom and told her to come get her lying cheating daughter. He had packed up some of the babies' stuff and told me to take some things for the next couple of days. I got dressed for work and got the babies ready. He put them in the car seat and put them in the car. He kept my phone and as I got in the car, I couldn't even look at my mom. I called E and told him what happened. He was still at home with his wife and didn't answer. I finally talked to him and told him what happened and he said Cass had already called him. I would later find out they had talked face-to-face. My mom dropped the kids off at daycare and then me at work. She gave me her phone to use. I called and reported it lost and had the service cut off when I got to work. However, Cass had already gotten what he needed out of it. Around 11, I got a delivery of flowers that sent me into a tailspin. Cass never liked to send me flowers, he felt they were a waste since they would die. He would rather get something that would last.

On the card he spoke of making things better there was also a hint of more to come. I would find out later, he had upgraded my wedding ring, but I would never get that now. I couldn't believe what had happened. I moved in with my parents. Cass took the truck back he had given me and caved to give me the older Maxima he had because I needed a car for the kids. Within the month, E suddenly moved out of state. He had mentioned it before, but I didn't think he was serious. I would later find out that during that talk Cass told him he didn't blame him, but that it would be in his best interest if he never contacted me again and to move out of the city. I had been wrong and I should have left Cass. I felt that two wrongs definitely weren't right, but it made me feel better.

Honestly, I didn't even believe in monogamy at this point. As wrong as I was, I learned a lot about myself from E. Me and the twins stayed with my parents for a couple of months. There were a few times me and the babies would spend the night out there, but it was rare. He did allow me to get most of my stuff and the twins items. We were living out of boxes. My parent's house was small and we were all on top of each other, but we made it work. During this time, I was mainly functioning on autopilot. I was trying to maintain a routine and normalcy for the twins.

This strength and bounce back that God had graced me with was serving me well. I didn't have money on hand, so I had to go into one of my retirement accounts to buy furniture and get us a place to live. I debated with myself and tried to find another way, but this was the only way. It broke my heart to dip into that account. I was proud of the savings I was accumulating for my future. I had to realize that at least I had it to tap into and maybe at some point, I could put the money back. So with that, I found us a place to live. Cass allowed me to get the twins crib and other big items and even moved them into the house. He also gave me back the SUV.

At first, we were going through the motions. He would come to see the twins and we would chit-chat, sometimes have sex, sometimes not. I was still his wife of course. He even cut the grass. Things were still tense, while we navigated this time. One night he comes over and says he wanted a DNA test. What the what? But ok, I am confident. He says everyone has been whispering and he wants to be sure. I did not have a doubt and was confident so I agreed. Made the appointment and went and had mouths swabbed. Things slowly went on. A couple of weeks had passed and one night he came over to see the twins. We put them to bed and then he wanted sex. We had sex, had gotten up, and cleaned up. I had come out of the bathroom and was getting something off the bed. I had turned around and he had grabbed me by the throat and shot the cags up under me, (kicked my legs out from under me). I was on my back and didn't know what was going on. While choking me, he would pull out the DNA results and he is not the father. This would be the second time I would see him cry. He wanted to know if I knew. I told him I was crazy but not that crazy. If I had thought that the twins were not his, I definitely would not have stayed with him. He felt like his heart had been ripped from him. He loved the twins. I was in so much shock. The only saving grace I had was that it happened right before we had gotten back together when I had left him. Had it not been for that, I believe he might have beaten me severely. This would further strain an already strained relationship. Out of his hurt, he would waste no time and share this news. His ex Gina was all too quick to say I told you so, that his beloved was further fallen from grace. It would be a few weeks but he would decide that he did not know to not love the twins. So the twins were his and he would still care and love him like he had, like his other kids.

However, he was not going to grant me a divorce. I could stay in my house and we would continue on for now, but at some point, we would come back together. This would also begin a time when his temper would become short towards me. He didn't want me to reach out to their biological father. I did, but he didn't want anything to do with them either. He was now married and wasn't trying to explain that or the fact he didn't want any more kids. This was all right before the twins 1st birthday. Needless to say, I did not have a big party for the twins. It was so much going on, I did something small with my parents. After about six weeks, Cass was arrested in a glorified fashion that once again had his life playing out on all the major news outlets. His home was raided, my parents home was raided, and all our cars were taken except for the truck I had. They didn't come to my home thank God, nor was I included in the indictment.

They had been watching him for months. Started right after he had put me out. Cass wasn't worried and told everyone else to not worry. I was worried, worried about what would have happened if me and the twins were there. I could have lost my babies and ended up in jail with him. He dismissed me, but it was the truth. I hated how I left that house, but I thank God I wasn't at the house. I thought I had dodged a major bullet and I did, but I wasn't clear yet as time would tell. He was locked up for a couple of weeks then finally out on bail.

During this time, I began to have anxiety attacks and fall into a deep depression. However, it would not allow me to stop. I had the kids that had to get to daycare and me to work every day. The daycare workers were whispering, my coworkers were whispering. Even the people at the church were all whispering and trying to understand who I had married and what I had gotten myself into. I was barely holding it all together. I would cry dropping the kids off at daycare. Cry driving, cry at home. I would always put on a brave face in front of the babies, at work, around everyone. I didn't want them to pick up on my despair. But when they were in bed or I was alone, I would literally break down. My mom and sister were worried about me. My pastor wanted to help me move out of the state and go on the run, go into hiding or move far away to get away from Cass.

As worried and scared as I was, something in me would not let me run. The economy was not good and I had a good job that was the only thing keeping my mind halfway sane, and I had these two young babies. Where would we go? I can't give up a job, I have to provide for these kids and I am not leaving without them. No, I would walk this tightrope until something gave. At some point, something would give. And now he has this court case that is more pressing. And of course, he still had his girlfriends. All I can say was that it had to be God. At this point, I had stepped down from being the nursery director at church because my life was in shambles and I felt I needed to sit under the Word and work to get my life together. I had a foundation, but I would need to build more on that foundation if I was going to survive this stage in my life.

Over the next couple of months, it seemed as if any little thing would set him off. He was now fighting me more than he had in the previous 12 years we had been together. I would pull into my garage and stay in the truck with the doors locked until the door closed, watching all mirrors and looking around. One night in a rush to get out since the twins had gotten fussy, I didn't do this and he snuck in. He grabbed me by my hair and threw me around that garage like a rag doll. My blood and hair were everywhere. He told me to open the door to the house and I thought it was to continue the beating, but when I saw him go to the truck my heart began racing thinking of him leaving with my babies. He had gotten them out of the car seat and brought them into the house. Gave them a kiss and then he left. I had been growing my hair since before being pregnant and it was finally on my shoulders. After this fight, I had clumps missing.

That night a neighbor had called the police because they heard my screams in the garage. When the sheriff got there, I was surprised and nervous. I hadn't had a chance to clean myself up as I had gotten the babies in bed. He asked what happened and I told him I was fine. He said I didn't look fine. I told him I wasn't going to press charges and didn't need the state trying to do that as that would be worse on me. He informed me that he wasn't originally from here, he was from California and he understood. He had seen this often. He asked if I feared for my safety at that moment. I told him I didn't think he was coming back, nor did he have a key so I didn't plan to let him in.

He gave me his card and said that he would be on patrol tonight and would periodically drive through and if I needed him to call. He said the caller had told him a man had walked between houses to a street over. I explained yes, that is what he probably did. However, I never knew what car he was in so I couldn't tell him what he was driving. I took his card and thanked him for his kindness in this situation. I let him out and went to take a shower and go to bed. When I finally got to my beautician, he asked what happened. He could see the cuts and bruises on my neck as well. I told him I had gotten into a fight. He said with who? Without looking up, I said well let me correct that, I got beat down.

He again asked by who? I sat quietly as I tried to hold back my tears. I asked him if he could fix it. Reese had been my stylist since I was 17, I am now 30. He knew. He rubbed my shoulder and said it would be ok. He said he would have to cut it. I said ok, for years I had worn short hair. I was fine with that. From my shoulders to above my ear. That's how short we would have to go to make it cute. My hair would never truly be the same. And I would never again grow my hair out after that. At this point, I began having more thoughts of suicide. However, I could not fathom leaving the twins for Cass to raise. So then I began having thoughts of how to kill him. I still had one of my guns, and I even thought of trying to get poison. Nothing would pan out though. Fear, I was still paralyzed. And now on top of all of that, I had decided to start back in the MBA program.

I had dropped out of when I got pregnant. Why would I do that to myself? I don't know. I think I had too much free time on my hand to think and I didn't like the despair that was always on my mind. Keeping myself occupied with something else would alleviate that. My mom would help me watch the kids when I had class. I started out great, even made class president. The only black people in the class were myself and another guy named Mark. One night in October after a working group session for class, I get home and my mom is there and Cass comes over right after I get home.

He is polite and seems calm, but I know he is upset because I didn't answer his call earlier. I almost wanted to ask my mom to stay and not go, but I let her leave and walk her out. She pauses as if looking for me to ask. Searching my eyes, I give her a hug and tell her I will talk to her later. I say a prayer as I walk back into the living room. Cass is calm, but that means nothing. I would later realize he was waiting on my mom to drive away before starting this fight.

This would start with a slap and escalate from there. Of course, I would be choked. He knew I hated being choked because I had asthma. I hated that feeling of suffocation. Usually, he would choke me and stop, tonight he would not. He would sit on top of me on the floor and choke me until I passed out. The entire time I am fighting I am praying in my mind, reminding the Lord of the promise you gave my mom over my life that Satan could not kill me. Well, this here is Satan in the flesh. I don't know how long I was out, but I awoke to him still punching me, then he choked me again until I passed out. This time when I awoke he was off of me and laughing at me. He told me to get up and give him some head. Then he thought about it and was like, "Nah, give me some your throat probably sore."

As I walk him back down the stairs after sex, he asks if I want him to go and buy me a turtleneck since I have deep cuts on neck and bruises popping up. I hate turtlenecks and I hate them because I feel like they are choking me. Not to mention this is October and it is unseasonably warm this year. I say no. He said fine but what are you going to tell people? I said well you didn't care about putting them there, so I guess I shouldn't care about telling them you put them there. He thought I was lying. He knew how fiercely private and ashamed I was. He was right, but at this moment, this was when my fear would push me. My biggest fear was always to be choked to sleep. Well, now I had lived through that and felt empowered in some way. I did not die. The promise that God had given to my mother had now become the promise that I would hold onto. It became real to me.

God confirmed the promise still holds true for you, now that I am old enough to carry it on my own. I would no longer be ashamed. A few days later we had Hallelujah night at church. I had on a jumpsuit. Most people didn't notice or weren't going to say anything. One girl noticed and she asked. I told her Cass did it. She looked and hugged me. I told her I was ok. She was like it's still not right. I said you are correct. But no longer would I hide and protect him. Then someone walked up and we switched conversations. My mother didn't know what to do. She couldn't make me do anything, so all she could do was pray. Hell, that was all I was doing and going through the motions of life. The only joy I would have would be these beautiful babies I had been blessed with.

This would also be a source of my greatest frustration within myself. Knowing that my choices had set us on a path to be guests on Maury and Jerry Springer. I couldn't understand how God would let this happen? Why now? Why this way? Me and my birth control had been going strong for 10 years. Who I was fooling? It wasn't God, it was me. I made a choice and when you make a choice, you must be prepared to deal with those consequences. I had plenty of choices. I chose my husband. I chose who I laid down with. I chose to go back, all of this was on me. I would bring myself to a place of numbness. I would shut down most of my emotions before they would overtake me. I felt as if I was on the verge of losing my mind most days.

The panic attacks felt like heart attacks I suppose. My chest would get tight, pains in my chest and heart racing, hands clammy, me sweating, labored breathing...and nothing to do, but let it pass. I would try to calm myself down and control my breathing. Tell myself I was ok, I would be ok. I would pray for it to pass. They would last anywhere from 10 to 30 minutes. Like with migraines, I would try and push my way through. The months kind of went by. We settled into this new way of being. The fighting eased up, but the demand for sex did not. He continued to come and see the twins and spend time with them. Thanksgiving came and was uneventful. We went to my aunt's house. The next day Cass comes by. I'm changing the babies' clothes and he tells me I spoil Prince too much. I am like no I don't. He is like give me your phone, I say no. From there, an argument ensues...for why I have no idea. He was already in an ill mood when he got there.

Finally, after going back and forth, I ask him why are we doing this? We stay arguing. Things are so broken, let's get a divorce. He gets furious. I am not leaving him, I don't get to decide that. I am alive because he allowed me to live and since he has slowed down working he can raise the kids. He doesn't need me and they don't need me. So if I don't want to be with him I don't have to live. I prayed and asked the Lord, how are you going to get me out of this now?

It was at this moment I started thinking my only way out was going to have to kill him. This was going to come down to me versus him. I told him I wasn't in love with him anymore and he didn't care. I told him I didn't want to be with him and he didn't care. And the crazy thing was I had seen messages from three new girls on his phone along with the few he had been messing with. This confused me more. Yet it didn't make a difference to him. This was a power struggle. I had to play this out. Lord, please show up soon! The twins loved him and he loved them. My year lease was coming up for renewal and although I loved the house, I was in a financial burden.

Cass was only minimally helping with daycare costs and now I was responsible for an entire household myself. The money I had pulled out of my IRA was long gone. The house I had grown up in was empty. My dad kept saying he was going to sell it or rent it, but it had been over two years and was still empty. My mom finally convinced him to fix it up and let me move in. However, it would take months and they would not let me renew for a short-term lease, so I decided to move back in with my parents until the house was done. So on a cool April day, some guys from the church came and loaded my furniture and big items into a POD.

I packed up some of their toys and most of our clothes in boxes. The POD was moved to the empty house, so I wouldn't have to pay to move it again. With the bare minimums, we moved into my parents. I had gotten a small crib from a family friend for Prince to sleep in and Princess could sleep in the playpen I had since she was the smaller of the two, but also the climber of the two. We were literally living out of boxes. At this time, I also put the twins in a new preschool. It was farther out, but much cheaper. It was also faith-based, which

I liked to help continue building the foundation I was trying to instill in them. Cass wasn't consistent in helping me pay their tuition and I was constantly behind. That added stress on me and my finances and although I was sad to pull them out, I knew it was the best for us all.

While staying with my parents, Cass would come and spend time with the twins. He would also demand for me to come and see him. The house we had once shared had burned to the ground over Christmas. Cass was back and forth between his mom's house and a new girlfriend in Decatur. He didn't think I knew about that and tried to say it was an Aunt, but I knew better than that. So here I am leaving my parent's house late to meet him at his mom's house. I wouldn't leave until after the twins were in bed. Some days he would want me to meet him on my lunch break. We would either use his brother's room that he now used or his mom's room. One night as I was leaving my mother went fussing about me leaving. I was tired and finally told her if I don't go to him he will come here and act a fool. He doesn't care about you or dad and I don't know what he will do, but I will not risk a fight escalating to a shootout, and you, dad, or the twins caught in crossfire all over something that could have been prevented.

Looking back I don't know if my dad ever knew and I never thought he would ever stand up to protect me from Cass. Me and my mom shielded him from so much, we never gave him the opportunity to defend his only child. Either way, I knew how volatile Cass could be and it was a chance I wasn't willing to take. I was still living gripped by fear. All I knew was that I would have to play this out. I once asked what the purpose of this was. He said he wanted me back, he wanted us to try. I didn't want to try. It wasn't worth it. He didn't care. He told me if I left him, he would kill me. He would kill me himself and he wouldn't care who was around. I was so tired and trapped. I couldn't believe he was still like this. All of this was taking its toll. I barely had energy for anything. Panic attacks were more frequent, I wasn't sleeping, I now had IBS, frequent migraines and yet I held it together for my kids. I had to, but I wasn't sure how much longer I could go. I had met with a lawyer to see what my options were. She advised me to wait and see how his court cases would go. I had explained to her that a restraining order would do no good for me. The only thing that could protect me was God. She agreed.

The twins 2nd birthday was fast approaching and he wanted to have a big party. So we had a party, a bounce house, tons of food and even four cakes. Yes, four cakes. I had already had my friend make one for each, Dora and Diego. But a church member had also made cakes as gifts after I raved on one of her cakes. It was a great day with family and friends. Cass, his mom, and oldest son came and I remember it being a nice day. In September, Cass went to court and not much came out of it. In October, Cass got picked up by the feds. I had seen him the day before. He was supposed to be going to Atlanta to work on some music. I knew when I hadn't heard from him in three days something was up. I finally got that collect call and he told me what happened. He was confident he would be out soon though. However, he would soon realize the feds didn't operate like the county did. I wouldn't see Cass in person again for another six months at his trial in March.

Now ironically, as things would happen the following week from his arrest, my dad finished the work on the house. A week later I moved in. I wouldn't even tell Cass I had moved for another couple of months. I had already had a post office box and I had told him to send any mail there. I was so excited to move into my own place again. I wasn't fond of the house and the memories it held, but I pushed past that to do what I needed to for my kids. For us, it was Heaven though. Kids were glad to get back into their own big beds and have all their toys. I was glad to have my own space and get back into our regular routine. Woosah...however, now God was about to begin a work I wasn't prepared for.

The next few months were calls back and forth as Cass had me making calls and appointments to lawyers and insurance companies about the case and our house that burned. But this time, I was free. I hadn't been this free from him in 10 years. He was not around to hover. At first, I assumed he would be home soon, but by December the courts denied him bail. He would be there until his trial. As the days turned into weeks, something started to happen. I began to breathe. This was the first time in 15 years that he couldn't hover over me. I was free to move and not necessarily be tied to my phone. I began to reevaluate my life and wonder how I ended up here?

What happened to my life? I peeled back the layers of me to understand what went wrong. I began to unpack issues from my childhood, and high school years, and early 20s that affected how I ended up here. This was a process that took years though. There were some dark days for me. I had to wait until I knew that he was going to be in jail for some time before I filed for divorce. Also, as his wife, there were certain legal protections I had during his court cases. Oh yea, your girl got subpoenaed and had to show up to court. Feds were threatening me to testify and everything. However, there was nothing I could prove, and a lot I didn't know. I was not part of his business. The one thing we had always agreed to. If he got more than seven years, I was not obligated to stay. So when his sentence came down, I waited a month or so, and then I filed for a divorce. I reminded him of what we had agreed to and that it was time for us to end. We were not good together. He was not happy at first, but he did agree and signed the divorce papers. He was not giving up his kids though. Now whether that was right or wrong at this point, it is what it is. He is the only father the kids know. He is a good father, only a terrible husband. It would take over a year before our divorce would be finalized.

REFLECTIONS

So that is how I got out. I would not necessarily suggest that anyone else take the course of action that I took. In fact, I probably would tell someone to go to a shelter. The one thing I would definitely stress is having a plan. My plan was simple, I knew him. I knew how to bide my time and keep the tensions down. I prayed, relied on my faith and God reassured me that I would be ok. He would tell me to hold on. Was it easy? HELL NO! It was hard. I would get panic attacks because I was under so much stress and yet no one knew I wasn't ok. There was no one to cry to or share with. I was ashamed. But most importantly, I didn't want anyone else to be in harm's way. So for three years, I lived in terror. Even after he was gone, I would wake up sweating, having nightmares of him coming after me, or even reliving the real-life horrors. I did talk to a therapist occasionally and that would always help. I cried. I screamed. I prayed. I studied. I looked hard at myself and made decisions. All to grow and heal. I had to be the best mom, sister, friend, and employee that I could be.

Without a shadow of doubt, only God saved me those nights when I should have been dead. When I should have lost my mind from my own thoughts, God kept me. I can't tell you who all had been praying for me, but I know that their prayers kept me. My children saved me. They kept me from giving up. They didn't ask to be here, but they were here and I was not going to let them down. Everything was to make a better life for them. And it was hard. Money was tight for a long, long time. I had to work two jobs to make it. But we made it. And now I am giving back. I became a crisis counselor, a domestic violence advocate, and a sexual assault advocate. I understand because I have lived through it.

Many people may think I was stupid and I am often asked why I didn't leave? It was never that easy. I thought love was supposed to hurt. Love had hurt most of my life. I was damaged. I accepted his flaws and signed up to deal with them. So how was I going to leave when it was a little more than what I bargained for? I needed to not do things to get him upset. This was my mentality and my reality. I thought this was what love was and this was as good as it was going to get. Honestly, we had been together too long to not work even if we weren't supposed to ever be together. It wasn't until I understood what healthy real love should be and that I deserved that, would I get free.

Regardless of what I had been through or what I had done, I still deserved to be treasured, appreciated, adored, protected and loved unconditionally. And sir/ma'am, so do you! Love does not have to hurt! So whatever you have gone through in your life, you deserve the same. And most importantly, we deserve peace. If you don't have peace at home, then you don't have peace at all. Everything you have gone through, you can use. I didn't ask to go through this, but I survived and it allowed me to find my purpose. The things that cause us the most pain are usually the things that will birth our purpose. Heartache, pain, trauma, you name it, we all have gone through something. What is it that you have gone through in your life? Are you using it to push you into doing something or are you using it as an excuse as to why you can't?

What are you doing to cope with the pain instead of healing from it? Sex and alcohol were my coping mechanisms until I decided to get healed. At some point, you have to know that what happened to you is not what defines you. You can't keep using what happened to you as a reason for why you do the things you do. If you recognize what causes you to do what you do, then you can begin to heal and begin using healthy alternatives and becoming whole. Turn the pain into purpose. Allow what you have survived to help someone else survive. You matter your voice matters. Therapy, God, and a few good friends can help you. Will it be easy? No, but it will be worth it? YES! Here is one of the scriptures that got me through:

Psalms 23

The Lord is my shepherd; I shall not want.
2 He makes me to lie down in green pastures;
He leads me beside the still waters.
3 He restores my soul;
He leads me in the paths of righteousness
For His name's sake.

4 Yea, though I walk through the valley of the shadow of death,
I will fear no evil;
For You are with me;
Your rod and Your staff, they comfort me.

5 You prepare a table before me in the presence of my enemies; You anoint my head with oil; My cup runs over.
6 Surely goodness and mercy shall follow me
All the days of my life; And I will dwell[a] in the house of the Lord
Forever.

HELPLINES

If you or someone you know is experiencing domestic violence call the national hotline 1-800-799-7233(SAFE) to talk to someone or 911 if you are in immediate danger.

For children, teens, and young adults in abusive relationships text "LOVEIS" to 866.331.9474 or call 866.331.9474 or visit loveisrespect.org

If you are having thoughts of suicide or in crisis call the national hotline 1-800-273-8255 or text "HOME" to 741741.

Local numbers for calls or texts may also be available in your area.

Excerpt from "The Fight from Within"

The night was going good. Fun times with my girls. Free drinks were even better. I was feeling good. Too good. Then it changed. As we got up to leave, it took all I had to straighten up and walk to the car. As crazy as it sounded, no matter how drunk I would get, I could always walk to my car like nothing was wrong. Tonight was no different, but when I got to my car I fell in. Thinking I needed a minute, but then realized I could hardly move. Head laying on my steering wheel. My girls are asking if I'm ok. I am mumbling, I'll be fine. Here comes that same old friend from the club and he was like she is good, I can take her home. I told my girl don't let him take me home. Something is wrong, very wrong...

Physically I was free. Emotionally, spiritually, and mentally I was still bound and broken. This fight would be an internal battle, more costly than the one I just came out of. This fight would be the most important of my life. How do you change what you believe about yourself? How do you change from unhealthy coping mechanisms to more healthy choices?

" *The Fight from Within*" by M'Shairi Bree .... Coming 2021

Made in the USA
Coppell, TX
05 December 2020

43075367R00049